WITHDRAWN

𝕮ornerstones of 𝕱reedom

The Story of
THE
CLIPPER SHIPS

By R. Conrad Stein

Illustrated by Tom Dunnington

5516

CHILDRENS PRESS, CHICAGO

Library of Congress Cataloging in Publication Data

Stein, R. Conrad.
    The story of the clipper ships.

    (Cornerstones of freedom)
    Summary: Discusses the design, uses, sailing,
and decline of clipper ships that enjoyed a short
but glorious reign of the seas during the mid-1800's.
    1. Clipper-ships—Juvenile literature.
[1. Clipper ships] I. Dunnington, Tom. II. Title.
III. Series.
VM144.S74   387.2'24   81-1299
ISBN 0-516-04612-8   AACR2

Copyright© 1981 by Regensteiner Publishing Enterprises, Inc.
All rights reserved. Published simultaneously in Canada.
Printed in the United States of America.

1 2 3 4 5 6 7 8 9 10 R 91 90 89 88 87 86 85 84 83 82 81

A generation before the development of the steamship, the world entered the "Golden Age of Sail." It was a time when tall sailing ships crowded into port cities. They flew the flags of a hundred different countries. Of those sailing ships one type stood taller, sleeker, and prouder than the others. She was the fabulous clipper ship—the queen of the Golden Age of Sail.

A clipper looked as if it had been carved by the hands of a sculptor. It was hard to believe it had been hammered together in a shipyard. Even the most seasoned sailor stopped what he was doing to stare at a graceful clipper skimming over the waves. From a distance, she looked like a sea bird gliding over the water. Up close, she was awesome—a giant of a ship built for speed.

This miracle of sail had its beginning in the mid-1800s. Americans at the time had developed a taste for tea.

Tea came from faraway China. It tasted better when it was fresh. But in the early 1800s it took American ships as long as six months to sail from a Chinese port to New York City. During those months, much of the expensive tea rotted in the ships' cargo holds. Ship owners asked designers for faster vessels. They needed ships that could deliver tea to American ports before it spoiled.

One of those designers was a young man named John Griffiths. He was a mathematical genius. To tackle the problem of building a faster ship, he used principles of science and higher math.

Griffiths knew that a knife would cut through water more easily than a cigar box would. So he planned a ship with a knifelike bow. Then he designed a very narrow hull. A narrower ship would glide through the sea more easily. But a narrow hull would reduce the ship's cargo space. So Griffiths made the new ship longer. Next he designed taller masts. He would cover them with sail to collect every little breath of the wind. Finally, he would remove everything from the deck that was not needed. A clear deck would lessen the wind resistance that slowed the speed of other ships. The

Rainbow

result of Griffiths' design was spectacular. He created a streamlined, towering ship called the *Rainbow*.

Historians disagree about exactly which ship was the first true clipper. At the time, other designers were building ships with slanting bows, narrow hulls, and tall masts. Historians do agree, however, that Griffiths' *Rainbow* was one of the first, if not the first, of the great American clipper ships.

The *Rainbow* was launched from New York in 1845. On her very first voyage she raced to Hong Kong and back with a load of tea in a little more than six months. It took older ships that long just to sail one way. The *Rainbow's* first voyage set a new speed record. It was also very profitable for her owners. The tea she carried earned twice what it had cost to build her. The owners immediately ordered another ship of the clipper design.

The next clipper designed by John Griffiths was even more remarkable than the first. She was a magic ship with a magic name—the *Sea Witch*.

Sea Witch

Launched in 1846, the *Sea Witch* was one of the largest ships of her time. She was as long as a city block. Her mainmast was higher than a thirteen-story apartment building. The *Sea Witch* was more than just a big ship. She was a creation of beauty and grace. The *New York Herald* called her "the prettiest vessel we have ever seen."

The early clippers amazed the world with their swiftness. Before clippers were built, people thought it was impossible for sailing ships to reach such speeds.

For hundreds of years, sailing-ship design had gradually improved. At the dawn of steam-powered ships, that gradual improvement reached its final step. Even today it would be difficult to construct faster sailing ships large enough to carry cargo. The designers of the clippers that dashed over the ocean one hundred and thirty years ago had achieved perfection.

The very name "clipper" signifies speed. In the 1800s, someone walking fast was said to be "going at a good clip." The new ships were called clippers because their designers expected them to cross the oceans at a good clip. They performed even better than their designers had dreamed.

The new American ships needed favorable winds in order to sail. It took another American to tell ship captains where to find those winds.

Matthew Fontaine Maury was a Tennessee farm boy. He joined the United States Navy at an early age and served at sea for ten years. Then he was given a desk job at the Bureau of Charts and Instruments. There the logs of navy ships were stored. Those logs were the diaries of ships. The navy considered the old logs to be junk. But to Maury they were a treasure. Navigation had always fascinated him. The logs gathering dust at the Bureau contained navigation information from hundreds of ships that had sailed millions of miles.

It had long been known that in some areas of the world the wind blew almost constantly. Other areas had little breeze. Maury studied the old logs. He hoped to draw maps showing which areas had the constant winds and which areas were calm. He once wrote, "The calm belts of the sea, like the mountains on the land, stand mightily in the way of the voyager, but, like the mountains on the land, they have their passes and gaps."

After poring over the logs, Maury published a

book called *Charts and Sailing Directions*. It contained maps and charts that showed the best routes to Europe and South America for every month of the year. The book was published in 1847. At first only a few ship captains read it. Those who did follow Maury's recommendations discovered that they reached their destinations in record time.

In a few years, Maury's book was used by all sailing-ship captains. The swift American clippers, armed with the knowledge in *Sailing Directions*, soon set sailing records that never would be equaled.

About a dozen American clippers were built. They streaked to and from China. On the trips back, the holds were full of tea. To advertise that the tea was fresh, some of it carried the label DELIVERED BY CLIPPER. Besides the tea trade, there seemed to be few other uses for the swift new ships.

Then, in 1848, a California ranch foreman saw something shining in the bottom of a river. He looked again. Gold! The California Gold Rush was on. That mad scramble to California started a clipper-ship building boom.

From all over the world, people hurried to California seeking fortunes. Prices there skyrocketed.

A barrel of flour that cost four dollars in New York sold for forty dollars in San Francisco. In Philadelphia, a tin of sardines cost a few pennies. It could be sold to a California gold miner for sixteen dollars. Homesick miners in California would even pay a dollar for a four-month-old copy of a newspaper from back East.

Merchants in the East wanted to rush their goods west to take advantage of prices gone wild. Hopeful gold miners wanted to race to California before the gold was mined out. Clippers did not carry many passengers. But the ships were so fast that clipper captains could demand very high prices for tickets to California. It took older ships two hundred days to sail from New York to California by way of Cape Horn. The sleek new clippers cut that time in half.

In the East, ship owners went into debt to cover the cost of building new clippers. And why not go into debt? The profit from a clipper's first voyage to booming California could more than pay for the ship's construction. Any later voyages brought pure profit for the owner.

Because of the California gold strike, more clippers began rolling out of the shipyards. In 1850,

twenty new clippers were built. In 1851, forty more were launched. The following year, sixty-six new clippers set sail. One hundred twenty-five sleek new clippers slid down launchways in 1853.

Boston builder John McKay owned a famous shipyard that built clippers. The very first clipper built by McKay was called the *Stag Hound*. She was launched in 1850. Her bow was so sharp and her hull so narrow that many old seamen thought she would topple over as soon as she hit the water. She did not topple over. Instead, she joined the race to California. The *Stag Hound* started a tradition of proud and sturdy clippers built in the yards of John McKay.

McKay was more than just a builder. He became a creator of masterpiece clippers. In his yards, the art of building sailing ships reached perfection. His ships will be remembered always in stories, songs, paintings, and poems. Out of Boston rolled graceful clippers with romantic names—the *Flying Cloud*, the *Westward Ho*, the *Lightning*. His ship *Great Republic* was the largest wooden merchant ship ever built. The *Sovereign of the Seas* also came from McKay's shipyard. One newspaper called her the "longest, sharpest, most beautiful ship in the world."

Launchings became exciting events in East Coast cities. Ship owners poured free champagne for dignitaries. They hired bands to play loud, brassy music. Schools often closed on launching days. Thousands of men, women, and children gathered at the dock to watch. They cheered when a spanking new clipper rolled down the ramp and splashed into the water.

Poet Henry Wadsworth Longfellow was a ship buff. He attended every launching he could. In one of his poems, Longfellow described the thrill of seeing a new clipper ship being launched:

> She starts, — she moves, — she seems to feel
> The thrill of life along her keel,
> And, spurning with her foot the ground,
> With one exalting, joyous bound,
> She leaps into the ocean's arms.

The sight of a graceful clipper moved some people to write poetry. It inspired others to paint. A clipper ship, with billowing sails and sweeping bow, was a perfect subject for brush and canvas. Some superb American paintings of the mid-1800s were exciting scenes of clippers cutting through the waves under a cloud of sail.

But clippers were not built to inspire poets and artists. They were built to speed freight over the ocean. Speed was the watchword of the clipper-ship era. Speed to carry goods and gold seekers to California. Speed to bring tea home from China. Speed to outrun the pirate ships that still operated near Malaysia. Speed to race over the trade routes and bring the world closer together than it ever had been before.

Using Maury's book, daring clipper captains streaked from port to port. The speed of their trips amazed the seafaring world. In 1848, the *Sea Witch* sailed from Hong Kong to New York in seventy-four days. She set a record that was never equaled. In 1851, the *Flying Cloud* raced to San Francisco from New York in eighty-nine days and twenty-one hours. Eighty-nine then became the magic number that other captains tried to better. Three years later the record was broken. The *Comet* flew from New York to San Francisco in an astonishing seventy-six days. Incredibly, more than one hundred years ago, sailing ships crossed the Atlantic with cargo in less than two weeks. Steamships would not attain such speeds until a quarter of a century later. In 1854, the greatest sailing record of all was established. The clipper *Champion of the Seas* logged a one-day run of 465 nautical miles. That meant the ship averaged close to twenty miles an hour. Few cargo-carrying steamers today can do as well.

A story in the early era of clipper-ship sailing told of a ship owner who watched his clipper leave New York. She was bound for Liverpool, England. Four weeks later, the ship owner was told that his clipper had returned to New York Harbor. The man was disappointed. He thought his ship had run into a gale in the middle of the Atlantic and was forced to turn back. The owner was astonished when the captain handed him Liverpool receipts and asked for his next assignment.

Sadly, clippers were also used on illegal runs. Often clippers carried opium from India to China. They carried slaves from Africa to the West Indies. Their speed made these voyages highly profitable.

A new breed of captain commanded the clipper ships. One historian called him a "daredevil with a mania for speed." In the past when a ship ran into a storm, the captain would reduce sail. He would leave only enough sail aloft to keep control of the ship. The clipper captain changed that practice. Because of his mania for speed, he kept his ship at full sail even in the teeth of a storm. To the clipper captain a storm meant wind. And wind meant speed. A clipper was built for speed, so he used all his sail. Only when the wind seemed about to tear the masts off the ship would he bring down his sails.

The greatest test of the nerve of a captain and the strength of a ship was the voyage around Cape

19

Horn. There the ship had to fight mountainous waves. Winds at Cape Horn were so powerful they could lift a man off the deck and blow him into the sea. While rounding the tip of South America, hundreds of ships were blown off course. Dozens of them were dashed to pieces on the rocks or on icebergs. Over the years, sailors gave names to the rocks and snags that had been the graveyards of ships and crews at Cape Horn: Deceit Rock, Desolation Island, Famine Reach, Useless Bay, Last Hope Inlet.

To a seaman, rounding "the Horn" was a nightmare. Still the clipper captains raced recklessly around Cape Horn. Keeping their ships at maximum sail, they challenged the forces of nature. They seemed to ignore the dangers of wind and treacherous rocks. One passenger whipping around the Horn on the *Sovereign of the Seas* wrote, "It was fearful to see the topmasts bend. We hardly dared to look aloft lest we should see the fabric blown away."

A crewman on a clipper had a tough, dangerous job. Much of his work was performed high above the deck in the *rigging*. The rigging was a spider's web of ropes. They had to be tugged to raise and lower

SAN FRANCISCO

NEW YORK

CAPE HORN

sails. Even when the ropes became coated with ice, sailors hauled on them with frozen hands.

In rain, sleet, hail, and icy winds the crewmen climbed into the rigging to work among the sails. They were often sent aloft during furious gales. "One hand for yourself and one hand for the ship," went an old saying among sailors. A crewman dangling in the rigging knew that he could not make one wrong move. If he did, he might fall to his death on the deck. Or he might tumble into the ocean and be swallowed by the water.

Despite the hardships and dangers, sailors were proud to man the graceful clipper ships. Pride in his ship is a sailor's tradition.

In the case of the clipper, the pride of young America rode the waves with her new ships. For years, Europeans had looked upon Americans as merely rebellious younger brothers of the British. But now the Americans had built a fleet of the most beautiful ships the world had ever seen. American ships were dashing over the sea-lanes with dazzling speed. And American companies were taking away the high seas trade. Once that trade had belonged almost entirely to the British. At last the rest of the world had to recognize the genius of the new country in the New World. One ship owner even named his clipper the *Young America*.

At first, clippers were purely an American product. Englishmen called them "Yankee clippers." But their excellent design was soon being copied by others, especially the seafaring British.

In December of 1850, an American clipper called the *Oriental* docked at London. She was under the command of Captain Ted Palmer. Before entering the harbor, Palmer's crew had scrubbed the decks and pulled the sails as tight as a drum skin. The *Oriental* was the first clipper ever to dock in London. Palmer wanted her to be noticed. She was more than just noticed. She caused a sensation.

All over London, people told one another to go to the docks to see this wonderful new American ship. At the docks, Londoners looked in awe at the *Oriental.* They gazed in wonder at her sharp, slanting bow, her slim hull, and her masts that towered high above neighboring ships.

The British public was amazed that such a magnificent vessel could be built in America. After all, the country was just seventy-four years old. English

Oriental

seafaring tradition went back hundreds of years. Why hadn't the English built lovely clippers like this one? London's famous newspaper, the *Times*, called for British ship builders to race into clipper construction. "We must run a race with our gigantic and unshackled rival," said a *Times* editorial as the *Oriental* lay at anchor. "It is a father who runs a race with his son. Let our ship builders and employers take warning in time."

Once they began a clipper program, the skilled British builders produced a fleet of handsome, swift clipper ships.

At the height of the clipper-ship era, captains often held races with each other. The owner of a winning ship rewarded her captain and crew with a bonus. The races became doubly important because of side bets made by the sailors of rival crews. The most famous ship race in history was staged by British clippers. It was called the Great Tea Race of 1866.

The contest started when five fast clippers left China bound for London. Ninety-nine days and 15,000 miles later, the two leading ships were the *Ariel* and the *Taeping*. They met in the English

Channel. There they started a dash to London that held the city spellbound. Spotters along the coast watched the progress of the two ships. They sent telegrams to London newspapers. In huge headlines the newspapers announced which ship was in the lead. Nearly everyone in London had a wager on the outcome of the race. The two ships hugged the coast. They stayed within a stone's throw of each other. Finally, the *Taeping* inched ahead of the *Ariel* and was declared the winner. The wildest and most closely followed race in clipper-ship history was over.

The reign of the clipper was short but glorious. From 1850 to 1870 she was queen of the seas. She was a ship of unmatched beauty. She streaked from port to port so fast that the world held its breath. But her time had to end. First, the California trade declined when the gold there was mined out. Next, freight rates dropped in 1857 because of an economic depression in the United States. Only six new clipper ships were launched that year. Significantly, one of them was named the *Twilight*.

In the 1870s, steam-powered ships emerged. At first, steamers operated only on inland waterways. Then, oceangoing sailing ships were fitted out with engines and paddle wheels. Finally, steamers that

could cross the Atlantic on their own power were developed. Those plodding steamers, belching smoke, ended the Golden Age of Sail.

Because the steamers did not depend on wind, they were almost always on schedule. Maury's book *Sailing Directions* advised sailing-ship captains where they should find favorable winds. But no book could create winds when the forces of nature silenced them. The winds that drove the clippers were fickle. At times they flung the ships across the water, whisking them past the steamers. At other times the ships entered what was called the *doldrums*. This was an area where there were no winds. In the doldrums, the mighty clippers drifted with drooping sails while steamers chugged past them.

A few clippers continued to sail after the turn of the century. Most of them, however, disappeared long before that. One by one, their brass and iron parts were stripped and sold for scrap. Their wooden hulls were either sunk or burned. Some clippers suffered an even more humiliating fate. They were demasted and hollowed out. Then their empty hulls were loaded with coal. They were towed by tugboats to and from dockside coal yards. The finest sailing ships ever built were being used as scows.

Only one clipper had an unusually long life span. Amazingly, she was still sailing as a merchant ship in 1922. She was then an old lady of fifty-three. While in service for a Portuguese shipping company, the clipper visited Falmouth Harbor in England. There she was spotted by a retired British sea captain. He promptly bought her for a few thousand dollars. The ship had been sailing under the Portuguese name *Ferreira*. But the retired captain knew she was really the British-built *Cutty Sark*— once one of the proudest clippers in the English fleet.

For many years, the ex-captain used the *Cutty Sark* as a training ship for the naval school he owned. Aboard her, young Englishmen learned the art of sailing. In 1952, the *Cutty Sark* retired from sea duty. She was restored to look exactly as she had during her glorious days as a clipper. She now rests in dry dock at the Greenwich, England, waterfront. Visitors climb on board to examine this superb sailing ship. The *Cutty Sark* is the last clipper ship left on earth. The hundreds of others that once raced over the sea-lanes vanished long ago.

Cutty Sark

Many visitors to the *Cutty Sark* like to imagine themselves back in the Golden Age of Sail. How exciting it must have been to watch lovely ships like this one slip away from dockside. When the captains raised the sails at the mouth of the harbor, the wind filled them like huge, fluffy pillows. Masts strained and yardarms creaked as the great ships raced like silent giants into the open sea.

What a magnificent sight it must have been!

About the Author

R. Conrad Stein was born and grew up in Chicago. He enlisted in the Marine Corps at the age of eighteen, and served for three years. He then attended the University of Illinois, where he received a Bachelor's Degree in history. He later studied in Mexico and earned a Master of Fine Arts degree from the University of Guanajuato.

The study of history is Mr. Stein's hobby. Since he finds it to be an exciting subject, he tries to bring the excitement of history to his readers. He is the author of many other books, articles, and short stories written for young people.

About the Artist

Tom Dunnington divides his time between book illustration and wildlife painting. He has done many books for Childrens Press, as well as working on textbooks, and is a regular contributor to "Highlights for Children." Tom lives in Oak Park, Illinois.